Why this book?

- Do you or does a loved one suffer from ir abdominal pain, or irritable bowel syndr

- Have you been recently diagnosed with gastro-oesophageal reflux disease (GORD) or any other digestion-related condition?

- Are you wondering whether you have a food allergy or intolerance?

This book covers the entire digestive system, from one end to the other. It provides clear, concise, and accurate information, and explains

- how the digestive system works
- what goes wrong and why
- the simple steps you can take to help yourself
- the symptoms that you must ask your GP to look at.

Checking out any troubling symptoms with your own GP is very important, and this book is not intended to be a substitute for doing so.

This book is dedicated to the memory of my dad, Tom, whose love of good food almost singlehandedly kept antacid manufacturers in business.

First Steps
to living with
Digestive
Problems

Dr Simon Atkins

LION

Text copyright © 2016 Simon Atkins
This edition copyright © 2016 Lion Hudson

Published by Lion Books
an imprint of
Lion Hudson plc
Wilkinson House, Jordan Hill Road,
Oxford OX2 8DR, England
www.lionhudson.com/lion

ISBN 978 0 7459 7041 7
e-ISBN 978 0 7459 7042 4

First edition 2016

Acknowledgments
Drawings pp. 27, 35, 64 © Sam Atkins

A catalogue record for this book is available from the British Library

Printed and bound in the UK, May 2016, LH26

Contents

Introduction

Everywhere you look in the media it seems that someone is cooking something. Television schedules are stuffed full of programmes in which celebrity chefs whip up delicious meals in their bespoke kitchens, and game shows where contestants compete to see who's baked the most mouth-watering cake or pastry.

And if that's not enough, we're also served up a growing variety of books, magazines, Sunday supplements, and websites solely devoted to food and how to turn it into the tastiest dishes possible. In fact, you can't move in a bookshop or supermarket these days without bumping into shelves jam-packed with the latest volumes of recipes by well-known cooks and resting actors.

On Amazon's UK website there are currently, in March 2016, 11,651 books on baking, 2,652 about barbecues and an incredible 28,219 books about national and international cookery. So whether you want to create the perfect pavlova, dish up roast potatoes to die for, or make a bowl of spaghetti alla puttanesca just like Mamma makes, there's a book to tell you how.

But despite our obsession with all things culinary, there are incredibly few books devoted to what happens next, when that delicious mouthful of food, having been savoured and chewed, is finally swallowed into the digestive system. And there are just as few devoted to those diseases of our bowels that can plague so many of us and turn the loveliest of meals into our next episode of belly ache, wind, indigestion, or diarrhoea.

This book aims to help to redress that balance.

Of course, while what goes into our mouths is not only the stuff of, but also an appropriate topic of conversation for, the dinner table, what comes out the other end is most probably not. And most of us are very grateful that the processes that churn tonight's dinner into tomorrow's trip to the toilet go on unnoticed, deep inside us.

But all of us, even the Queen and David Beckham, have to take a poo. And whether we like to talk about it or not, it's important to be aware of how our food gets from table to toilet, and what can go wrong in between.

There are quite a few conditions affecting our digestive systems that are worth knowing about, either because they are common and debilitating or because they are potentially life-threatening. And because many are treatable and may even be preventable.

As we work our way through the gut from top to bottom, we will look at some of the problems I see most often in my consulting room, including:

- indigestion, reflux, and stomach ulcers
- gallstones
- coeliac disease
- irritable bowel syndrome
- inflammatory bowel disease
- diverticular disease
- cancers
- piles.

We will look at their symptoms, what causes them, the treatments available, and ways in which to either minimize their effects or fend them off altogether.

It will come as no surprise that the foods we eat and the drinks we consume play a big part in not only triggering but also exacerbating digestive problems, so there's a fair amount of dietary advice included in these pages too. And while there are no actual recipes in the book, I hope there's plenty of food for thought.

We begin in Chapter 1 by following the journey taken by our food as it negotiates its way through our digestive system and we absorb its nourishment.

First Steps to living with Digestive Problems

1

The mechanics of digestion

Digestion is, according to the dictionary, the process by which food is broken down in the alimentary canal (one of the fancier aliases of the digestive system) into substances that can be absorbed and used by the body. In other words, it's the term that describes how we turn our food into its constituent chemicals so that they can refuel, build, and repair our body's tissues.

In order to understand this process – and also what can go wrong – it will probably help to take a quick trip along the alimentary canal itself to see what goes on where.

Basic bowel anatomy

The alimentary canal is actually more of a tunnel than a canal, and a dark, damp, and smelly tunnel at that. In an adult it is around eight and a half metres long and it runs from the lips at the top to the anus at the bottom.

A mouthful of food travelling along its length passes through the following sections: mouth, oesophagus (gullet), stomach, small intestine, duodenum, jejunum, ileum, large intestine, caecum, colon, rectum, and anus.

The small intestine is, paradoxically, the largest section. It is around 5 metres long and has to be coiled up in the centre of the abdomen to allow it all to fit in. The large intestine, on the other hand, is much shorter – about 1.5 metres long – but gets its name because it has a much wider diameter. It fits neatly around the edges of our insides, forming a three-sided frame for the small intestine.

Other organs involved in digestion, such as the liver and pancreas, lie alongside the bowel, with ducts that feed into it like tributaries into a much larger river. And the whole thing is wrapped in a meshwork of blood vessels which keep the bowels oxygenated and take away the absorbed nutrients so they can feed the rest of the body.

The digestive process

As it travels through the bowels, food is broken up both physically and chemically, and then absorbed in these different regions. The leftover waste is then expelled from the bottom.

Mouth

The process of digestion starts here as food is bitten and chewed into smaller pieces by the teeth, and squeezed and softened by saliva and the tongue. Saliva also contains a chemical enzyme called amylase, which begins breaking up larger carbohydrate molecules such as starch into smaller sugar molecules such as glucose.

Oesophagus

Not a lot happens in this very muscular tube, which is around 35 centimetres long and 2 centimetres wide. It is simply responsible for transporting the mushed-up food from the mouth to the stomach once it's been swallowed. The food is propelled downwards by rhythmical contractions of the wall of the oesophagus, in a process known as peristalsis.

At its bottom end is a region called the gastro-oesophageal junction (try saying that after a glass of Prosecco). This is where the digestive tract leaves the chest and enters the abdomen, and where food enters the stomach.

Stomach

Food from the oesophagus enters the stomach through a muscular valve called a sphincter, which keeps the food inside while it is digested further. A second sphincter at its exit lets out what's left after it's been sloshed around by further waves of peristalsis and had all the protein molecules in it broken up by the enzyme pepsin, with the help of industrial-strength hydrochloric acid.

Other enzymes also help to start breaking down fats, and the acid plays a role in killing off any infectious germs that have managed to make their way in. This acid is also potentially damaging to the cells lining the stomach itself, so they secrete a mucus coating which forms a protective layer.

Duodenum

Some four to six hours after being eaten, the digested food is squirted out of the stomach into the first part of the small intestine called the duodenum, a C-shaped tube around 30 centimetres long. Ducts from both the gallbladder and pancreas enter the duodenum, secreting bile (from the gallbladder) and a cocktail of digestive enzymes (from the pancreas) onto its contents.

Bile is produced in the liver and stored in the gallbladder, from where it is released at mealtimes via the bile duct into the duodenum. Here it breaks down fats into smaller fatty acids which can be absorbed. Fluid from the pancreas is also added at this point. It contains enzymes that help to break down carbohydrates, fats, and proteins.

By this stage the partly digested food is called chyme and has the consistency of a rather unappetizing smoothie with lumps in it. Chyme is very acidic and the pancreatic fluid also contains bicarbonate to neutralize it.

Jejunum

As the chyme flows downstream from the duodenum through the alimentary canal, it passes into the jejunum, the next section of the small intestine, which is around 1.5 metres long and is coiled up underneath the belly button. It's here that all the hard work of digestion that's gone on higher up in the gut starts to bear fruit as nutrients are absorbed from the intestines into the bloodstream.

The wall of the jejunum is covered in tiny finger-like projections called villi, which in turn have their own tinier finger-like projections sticking out from them, called microvilli. This provides a massive surface area over which absorption can take place, allowing digested molecules of protein and carbohydrate, as well as vitamins, to pass from the bowel into the surrounding blood vessels.

Ileum

This is the last and longest section of the small intestine, where all of the remaining goodness is absorbed from what's left of the chyme. This includes fatty acids, amino acids (protein building-blocks), vitamins, alcohol, sodium, and potassium.

After passing through what can be up to 4 metres of ileum, all that remains of the meal, now eaten many hours ago, passes into the large intestine.

Large intestine

The large intestine doesn't produce any enzymes but instead relies on an army of "good" bacteria to do the final work of digestion. It's thought that there are around 500 species of these bacteria in our large intestine and that if you dried out the contents of this part of the bowel, there would be 10^{12} (1 trillion) of them in every gram. These bacteria don't rely on oxygen to stay alive, so they are well adapted for hanging out in the airless depths of our insides.

Fermentation of chyme by these bacteria not only allows the release of any vitamins that have yet to be digested, but also turns it into its final incarnation: faeces. The main by-products of the fermentation process are the gases carbon dioxide and methane, which are often released to great embarrassment (or, for children, to great hilarity) as flatulence.

Then, finally, any waste that's left moves on from the colon into the rectum, from where it is literally dumped from the body, via the anus, down the toilet.

The whole digestive process from table to toilet, or perhaps plate to poop, varies not only from person to person, but from day to day for each of us. Studies of bowel transit show that the normal range is anything between 12 and 72 hours, depending on what's been eaten, with 48 hours being an average.

Everyone should open their bowels every day – otherwise, there is something wrong with them.

Not everyone will open their bowels every day, while for others it's not unusual to pop to the toilet more than once. If you go between three times per day and once every three days, you are considered normal.

2

Checking out the bowels

In this chapter we'll take a look at the kind of examinations and tests that you might be put through if you make an appointment to see your doctor about digestive symptoms. These tests will vary depending on which bit of your bowels seems to be causing trouble, with some being more invasive (not to mention embarrassing) than others.

Please don't let anything that follows put you off booking that appointment. Very often your GP will be able to put your mind at rest after listening to a description of your symptoms, having a quick prod of your tummy, and asking you to give a sample of blood or poo.

And even if something more technical is needed and you are advised to let someone poke a tube containing a camera up your bottom, the short-lived discomfort has got to be better than the alternative of missing something serious that could have been cured.

At the GP's surgery
As ever, you are most likely to book to see your family doctor in the first instance, to see if they can help work out what's going

on with your digestive system. They won't have any special gadgets, or X-ray eyes, to actually see inside you, but chances are they will have come across your problem many times before. So by taking a detailed medical history and carrying out a physical examination, they will be able to start making sense of things for you.

The medical history
Alongside fielding some general questions about your symptoms – such as when they started, how they progressed, and if anything makes them better or worse – you will also need to be prepared for a few questions about some of the more private moments in your life.

If you're British, this can come as a bit of a shock, as we are generally a bit straight-laced and not that comfortable discussing the intimate details of our bowel movements or the expulsion of bodily matter. But remember that the person asking the questions discusses these things for a living and will be very hard to embarrass, so be as open and honest about your symptoms as possible. After all, doctors are not mind readers and won't be able to help unless they have all the facts.

Don't get het up about what terms to use. Again, while the medical profession has invented some seriously odd words to describe the stuff that plops out of your bottom (I mean, *stool*!? I ask you!), but we would rather hear it in the terms you would normally use for these bodily functions. We're not prudish; we can take it!

So don't overthink what you are going to say. If when you go for a dump there's blood on the bog roll, just say that. If you puke every time you eat, tell us, and if, as one man told me, you pebble-dash the toilet bowl with the runs every day and only just make it in time, please don't keep it to yourself.

Once these pleasantries are out of the way, there'll be a few questions about whether your symptoms have happened before, if anyone in the family has had anything similar, and some enquiries about your diet before the interrogation is wrapped up. Then you'll be asked to head over to the examination couch for the next stage of the process.

The physical examination

Mythbuster

If there is something wrong with the digestive system, it will show up with a quick check of your stomach.
Many digestive problems have symptoms and physical signs that affect more than just the abdomen. There can be tell-tale signs of some conditions in the mouth and on the skin, so don't be surprised if these are checked out too.

Most of the examination will, though, involve scrutiny of your abdomen. The doctor will want to look at its shape, to see if there are signs of weight loss or distension, and they will also press around it to see if they can feel any lumps or internal organs, or provoke any pain anywhere. This palpation will cover the whole of your belly, with the doctor examining all four corners and around your belly button with the flat of their hands.

Finally, and depending on both your symptoms and cooperation, the doctor may want to examine your bottom. This might just mean a peek on the outside to eyeball any piles or tears in the skin around the anus, but it may also involve what's known in the trade as a PR (or *per rectum* examination, to use the Latin). Feeling inside the rectum will often provide vital information that can rule in, or rule out, certain diagnoses, including cancer, and so determine the speed at which further investigations or referrals need to be made.

I will always remember the words uttered to us as medical students by Bristol University's professor of surgery as he taught us about the importance of carrying out a PR: "If you don't put your finger in it, one day you'll put your foot in it!" It's a fairly unpleasant experience for both parties involved, but it can be vital, so if you do hear the snap of a latex glove as you lie anxiously behind the examination curtain, rest assured it's being donned for a good reason. And you can also rest assured that no one will do it without your permission.

Laboratory tests

Next, you may well find yourself being asked to have some blood, stool, or even urine tests.

Blood tests

The box below shows some of the main things your blood will be taken to check for.

Anaemia (blood loss in the bowel can be a feature of some digestive problems)

Inflammation (some conditions are caused by inflammation of the lining of the bowel wall)

Liver abnormalities (particularly if you have pain on the upper right-hand side of your abdomen, or you are jaundiced)

Coeliac disease (there's a specific test for this condition, which we will look at in more detail in Chapter 5)

Abnormalities in your blood protein, vitamin, or mineral levels (as these give the doctor information about whether your problem is affecting your general level of nutrition)

Lipase (an enzyme whose level rises with some problems with the pancreas)

Other tests may well be ordered depending on your symptoms, but those in the box above are likely to be checked first.

Stool tests
Checking a sample of this stuff will involve you collecting some in a special pot, which is then sent off to the lab. This process will have varying degrees of difficulty depending on your chosen method of collection, your manual dexterity, and your sample's consistency, not to mention the sensitivity of your nose to such substances.

But it is generally best to hold a large enough disposable container under your bottom while on the toilet and then either decant or scoop the required quantity of its eventual contents into the pot your doctor provided (most come with little spoons to help you). Always remember to attach the label and screw the lid back on tightly before popping it in the sample bag and delivering it to the laboratory collection point, which will often be at your surgery or health centre.

Finally, if you think all that was bad for you, spare a thought for the poor lab technician who has to open the pot at the other end, when its contents will no doubt have matured a little!

Tests on these samples will usually be aimed at tracking down any signs of infectious organisms if your problem involves ongoing diarrhoea, or the specific germ *Helicobacter pylori* if you have chronic indigestion (more on this in Chapter 3).

Urine sample
This is only likely to be checked if you have abdominal pain, to make sure the pain isn't coming from a kidney or bladder infection rather than from your gut. Women of child-bearing age with acute abdominal pain may also be asked to have a pregnancy test on their sample, again to make sure their pain

is from the bowel and not from an altogether different, and perhaps unexpected, source.

Endoscopy

An endoscope is a long, thin, flexible tube with a light and video camera, which can be used to look inside your digestive system from either end, or both if you're particularly unlucky. Doctors will often use the shorthand description for this kind of test as "having a camera popped inside".

An endoscopy looking at your stomach is referred to as a gastroscopy, while from the other end you will be referred either for a sigmoidoscopy or a colonoscopy, depending how far around the large intestine the specialist wants to see.

Gastroscopy

This test is carried out in hospitals or specialized community clinics, where it is used to examine the oesophagus, stomach, and down into the first part of the duodenum. Before attending your appointment, you will be advised about any tablets you need to avoid taking on the day of the test, and you will be given instructions about what you can and can't eat and drink.

The examination takes around 15 minutes to carry out and will involve the doctor or specialist nurse putting the endoscopy tube into your mouth and asking you to help it down into your stomach by swallowing. They will offer you an anaesthetic throat spray to make it easier; if you are really anxious about it, you can be given a sedative, which keeps you awake but ensures you're much less aware of what's going on.

If you choose the throat-spray option, you'll be able to watch what's going on in your own insides on a TV monitor. The specialists will take pictures and biopsy samples of your stomach and then you'll be taken to the recovery room where they'll explain their findings.

Afterwards, your own doctor will be sent a full report and any treatment or follow-up recommendations, which they will be able to go through with you a week or two later.

Sigmoidoscopy and colonoscopy

Given where the camera is going in these tests, the preparation is a little more complicated than it is for gastroscopy, to ensure the endoscopist can get a good view of your large bowel. As a result, not only will you be sent details of medicines to avoid taking before the tests and some specific dietary advice, but you'll also receive some sachets of a rather powerful laxative to give you a good clear-out.

Do not plan to go far from a toilet on the day you take this medicine.

A full colonoscopy will take between 30 and 45 minutes, whereas a sigmoidoscopy will be over in half that time. As with the gastroscopy above, you will be offered a sedative to make the procedure seem more comfortable.

Once on the examination table, you will be asked to lie on your left-hand side and the specialist nurse or doctor will pass the endoscopy tube into your anus, with the help of lubricating jelly, and then around your colon. Air will be pumped into your bowel to help them get a good view. Images will again appear on a screen in the endoscopy room and biopsies of the bowel wall may be taken.

After some time in the recovery room, you'll be given feedback on what's been found and a full report will be sent to your own doctor. If you've been sedated, you will need someone else to take you home.

Capsule endoscopy

This test is used when, despite having one or both of the types of endoscopy just described, doctors are still no wiser about your condition. It's particularly useful if the problem is felt to be in the small bowel, beyond the reach of a traditional gastroscopy.

The capsule itself has a colour camera, battery, and transmitter inside it. Although it's reminiscent of a horse pill, it can be swallowed quite easily. As it travels through the digestive system, it sends pictures to a recorder that is worn around your waist.

After eight hours you return to the hospital to have the recorder removed so the images it's received can be analysed. Meanwhile, the disposable capsule carries on its merry way and is eventually flushed down the toilet.

Scans

These mostly less invasive tests are also helpful when it comes to investigating digestive problems.

Ultrasound scan

This scan involves having a handheld probe placed on your tummy which, with the help of some rather cold gel that's squirted onto your skin, emits high-frequency sound waves into your abdomen. The signals that bounce back are picked up again by the probe, and a computer converts these signals into images.

This type of scan is particularly helpful for looking at your internal organs, rather than the bowels themselves, and is most commonly used to check out:

- the liver
- the gallbladder
- the spleen
- the kidneys.

Computed tomography (CT) scans

These scanners, which are shaped like large, white doughnuts, use X-rays to create images of your internal organs. To undergo the scan, you have to lie down on a flat bed, which the radiographer (who operates the scanner) then moves in order to position you under the doughnut so that the imaging process can begin.

The scanner doesn't cover you completely, so it isn't claustrophobic. And it's quite a quick examination, only taking around 20 minutes.

There are two ways that doctors might use a CT scanner to investigate your symptoms:

- *A straightforward scan.* This provides high-quality images of all your internal organs, such as your liver, spleen, pancreas, and kidneys, which can then be examined in thin slices.

- *A virtual colonoscopy.* This test involves having the same kind of bowel clear-out before your appointment as with a regular colonoscopy (see above). Then, in the X-ray department, you will have an injection of a dye into a vein in your arm, which will help to show up the lining of the wall of the bowel. To help further, the doctor will also insert a tube into your anus through which air is pumped. These measures will allow any tumours and polyps inside the bowel to be spotted.

3

Indigestion

Judging by the number of adverts on television promoting products that alleviate this condition, it's very familiar to many of us. And having recently reached the ripe old age of 48, I have very few contemporaries who don't experience the odd bout of indigestion every now and again. For me, it's invariably after I've over-indulged at dinner parties with friends, wolfed down some fast food while on the move, or tucked in to a late-night curry.

Mythbuster

Indigestion is just something you get as you age – nothing to worry about.
We shouldn't dismiss persistent indigestion out of hand as just something to be expected as we get older. Heartburn and reflux can be symptoms of some quite sinister problems, and it's important to be aware of when a quick slug of an antacid is appropriate and when you ought to let your doctor know about your symptoms.

In this chapter we will look at the often confusing terminology around indigestion, discuss its causes, and see what treatments are available.

What is indigestion?

As with all medical symptoms, we need to be sure that we are all discussing the same problem. And when it comes to indigestion, this can be difficult, as people have many different terms that they use to describe the same set of symptoms.

A quick internet search suggests the following commonly used words:

- Reflux
- Acid indigestion
- Gas
- Biliousness
- Heartburn
- Waterbrash

What they all describe, to one degree or another, is the symptom of a burning upper abdominal pain that often begins just below the lower tip of the breastbone (sternum), but can frequently travel up behind it. This pain commonly occurs in the hour or so after a meal, particularly a heavy one, and can be accompanied by a handful of other symptoms, including:

- feeling full up and bloated
- belching
- a sensation of watery acid, or even food, coming back into your mouth
- nausea and even, if extreme, vomiting.

Thankfully, although indigestion is a very common symptom, it's rarely either severe or serious, and generally just reminds us to have smaller portions, eat more slowly, and wash our meals down with less booze. But persistent indigestion can be a sign that there is more going on inside than just the effects of overindulgence and will warrant a trip to the doctor rather than to the medicine cabinet for yet another swig of antacid.

What are the causes of indigestion?

As we've already seen, indigestion is the name given to a symptom rather than a disease, and it has a large number of causes, ranging from drug side effects through to stomach ulcers, with many others in between. The ones discussed below by no means cover all of the possibilities but represent some of the most common.

Side effects of medication

There's quite a list of pills which, while doing you good by treating what they've been designed for, can mess with your stomach and leave you with an unwanted dose of indigestion as a side effect. These include:

- antidepressants, especially fluoxetine, citalopram, sertraline, and other selective serotonin reuptake inhibitors (SSRIs)
- antibiotics
- iron tablets used to treat anaemia
- tablets such as alendronic acid used to strengthen bones when treating osteoporosis
- medication for the heart, such as nitrate drugs.

But some of the biggest culprits are the so-called non-steroidal anti-inflammatory drugs (NSAIDs), such as aspirin, diclofenac, and ibuprofen.

These drugs can irritate the lining of the stomach and, if taken regularly for long periods, can cause the development of stomach ulcers.

If you have a history of stomach ulcers, then you will probably be advised not to take this type of painkiller. But even if you haven't, and particularly if you are either over 65 years old or going to be on them for a while, your doctor may prescribe you a medicine to protect your stomach while you are taking it. The most commonly used gastro-protector is omeprazole, which we will look at in the section below on treating indigestion.

Helicobacter pylori *infection*
Helicobacter is a bacterium that can infect the lining of both the stomach and the duodenum. It's believed that around 25 per cent of people in Europe, North America, and Australasia are infected with this bug, but that it only causes symptoms in 80 per cent of those who have it. The infection rate is much higher in people living in developing countries, bringing the average rate across the globe up to 50 per cent.

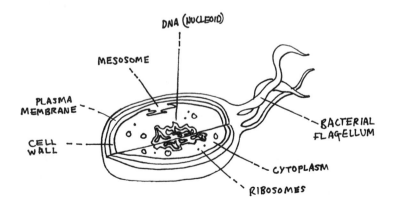

Know your enemy: The anatomy of a *Helicobacter* cell

Not only can it cause indigestion by inflaming the walls of the stomach and duodenum, but it is also known to be the most common cause of gastric ulcers.

> The research that led to the discovery of the role of *Helicobacter pylori* was carried out by two Australians called Barry Marshall and Robin Warren, who were awarded the Nobel Prize for Medicine and Physiology for their work in 2005. The proof that the bacterium was linked to the development of stomach inflammation came when, after a normal endoscopy, Marshall drank a sample of *Helicobacter*. When he was retested just eight days later, he was found to have an extremely inflamed stomach (gastritis). Best not try that at home, though.

Gastro-oesophageal reflux disease (GORD)

This occurs when acid from the stomach leaks upwards into the bottom end of the oesophagus. For many people this is the result of a faulty sphincter at the top of the stomach, for which there is no obvious cause. But it can be caused by a hiatus hernia (see below), smoking, eating big meals, obesity, and drinking high volumes of alcohol.

Hiatus hernia

Not to be confused with the type of hernia that pops up in the groin after a bout of heavy lifting, hiatus hernias occur inside the body and leave no visible tell-tale lumps on the outside. They are, as one of my professors told us at university, not a disease but an anatomical abnormality occurring when part of the stomach slips up through the hole in the diaphragm into the chest cavity.

The diaphragm is a big sheet of muscle that sits underneath our lungs, separating the contents of the chest from the abdomen. In its relaxed state, it forms a slight dome pointing up towards the head; when it contracts, it flattens out. This contraction happens each time we take a breath, helping to draw air into the lungs.

In the middle of the diaphragm there is a hole through which the oesophagus passes on its way down to join the stomach. A hiatus hernia occurs when part of the top of the stomach pushes up through this hole into the chest cavity. This can occur in one of two ways:

- *Sliding hiatus hernia*. The most common type, this occurs when the top of the stomach pushes directly through the hole and the oesophagus moves up with it.

- *Rolling hiatus hernia*. Here, part of the top of the stomach pushes up alongside the oesophagus.

As a result of this herniation, and particularly in the case of a sliding hernia, the valve at the top of the stomach is no longer as tight as it could be – having shifted upwards, it has lost the extra support it normally gets from the diaphragm itself. This allows acid from the stomach to reflux into the oesophagus, causing inflammation and pain.

My dad had a hiatus hernia, and when it gave him indigestion, he would say he had a dose of "stomach on the chest".

Stomach ulcers

Most people who come to see me in surgery with persistent indigestion are worried that they have an ulcer. Fortunately, these aren't as common a cause of indigestion as the problems listed above. They are also usually less severe than the one that afflicted Lord Grantham in a famous scene from the television series *Downton Abbey*, which burst midway through a formal dinner, spraying blood across the starched, white tablecloth.

Ulcers are basically open sores that occur in the lining of the stomach, oesophagus, and duodenum when there is damage to its protective outer layer. This damage is usually caused either by *Helicobacter* infection or by repeated use of NSAID medication.

Alongside indigestion, ulcers are likely to make people feel sick or nauseous, induce a sensation of quickly feeling full after even small meals and snacks, and sometimes cause weight loss. They can also bleed, with blood showing up in the motions, which often turn black, or in the vomit as with his Lordship at Downton.

Stomach cancer

This is a thankfully very uncommon cause of indigestion. Its other symptoms will include many of those caused by stomach ulcers, but it will also lead to weight loss and the development of anaemia. The chances of it being successfully treated are much higher if it is picked up early, which is another good reason to see your GP if you have symptoms of indigestion that don't settle with simple treatments. (See Chapter 10 for more on stomach cancer.)

How is the cause of indigestion investigated?

When you consult your doctor about ongoing indigestion, their approach to investigating it will follow the tried and tested routine of first taking a detailed medical history and then asking you to pop on the couch for an abdominal examination. It's only after this initial assessment that they will consider which investigations to pursue.

When taking the history, they will want to find out:

- the exact nature of your symptoms and whether there are any worrying features to these

- any factors that make your symptoms worse or better

 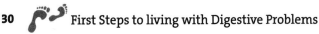

- how long you've had symptoms
- what remedies you may have tried yourself and whether they've helped or not
- if anyone in the family has had anything similar.

During the examination they will be checking to see if your tummy is tender anywhere, in particular when they press it, and whether they can feel any lumps that they shouldn't be able to.

If you are under 55 years old and have what seems like simple, straightforward indigestion, your doctor might simply discuss possible lifestyle changes with you, such as quitting smoking, adopting a healthier diet, and cutting back on your favourite tipple. They may then start you on some medication (see next section) and arrange to review your symptoms once you've tried it for a month or two.

They may also suggest that you have a test to check for *Helicobacter*. There are four common tests in use for checking whether you have this infection:

- *Breath test.* Here, the level of carbon dioxide in your breath is taken before and after you have a special drink containing a substance called urea. If you have *Helicobacter* in your stomach, the level will be higher after having the drink than it was before, because the bacteria break the urea down into ammonia and carbon dioxide.

- *Stool test.* You will be asked to collect a small sample of your poo, which is then tested for signs of *Helicobacter*.

- *Blood test.* This test is less useful than the others. Although it can identify if you have been infected with *Helicobacter*, it is not able to tell whether you have a current or past infection.

- *Biopsy.* A sample of the wall of your stomach is taken during an endoscopy and sent to the lab for analysis.

If, however, you have severe symptoms or your symptoms don't settle with appropriate treatment (see below), then you are likely to be referred for an endoscopy for a detailed assessment of your oesophagus and stomach.

Treatments for indigestion

The treatment you are given will depend on the severity of your symptoms, whether or not you are found to have *Helicobacter*, and the findings of an endoscopy if you have to have one.

Lifestyle advice

While the medicines below can help reduce symptoms, there are a few things you might be able to do to help yourself which, unlike pills, aren't likely to give you side effects.

- Eat regular meals and steer clear of wolfing down large portions, especially late in the evening.
- If you smoke, consider quitting.
- Cut down on the amount of alcohol you drink.
- If you are overweight or obese, then losing weight can certainly help.
- If your symptoms are worse at night, avoid food and drink at least a couple of hours before you go to bed and consider propping up the head end of your bed with bricks so that gravity will help the contents of your stomach stay where they should be.

Medication

With mild, intermittent indigestion and reflux, you can start by trying one of the wide variety of antacid sweets, chews, and liquids available over the counter. Your pharmacist will be very happy to advise you about these. If you have more severe symptoms, then your doctor has a number of treatments that they can prescribe to help:

- *Proton pump inhibitors (PPIs)*. This group of medicines, which have revolutionized the treatment of indigestion and reflux, include the drugs omeprazole and lansoprazole. They work by cutting down acid production by the cells lining the stomach and are used to treat symptoms and help clear up ulcers. The length of time you will be on one will vary according to your exact diagnosis.

- *H2 blockers*. The drugs in this group include ranitidine and cimetidine. They also reduce acid production but are not as strong as PPIs. They are often prescribed on their own but can be used alongside PPIs for particularly stubborn symptoms.

- *Helicobacter treatment*. If you are found to be infected with this bacterium, you will be given a combination of two antibiotics and a PPI to take for a week to eradicate it. You are then likely to be advised to continue with the PPI for a while longer until all your symptoms subside.

Surgery

If your symptoms persist despite all of the measures suggested above, then your doctor may suggest referral to a surgeon for a procedure called a Nissen fundoplication. This operation, which is usually carried out using keyhole surgery, involves the top part of your stomach being wrapped around the bottom end of your oesophagus to permanently tighten the valve and prevent stomach acid from refluxing back up into the gullet.

The procedure is carried out under general anaesthetic while you are asleep and takes between 60 and 90 minutes to perform. After the operation, you will be advised to eat soft or blended foods for the first six weeks, after which time recovery should be complete.

4

Gallstones

The gallbladder is a little pear-shaped sack that is anything from 3 to 6 inches long and sits underneath your liver in the right upper corner of your abdomen, just under your ribcage. Its job is to collect and store bile – a yellowy-green chemical made when red blood cells are broken down in the liver – and then squeeze this out through a duct (imaginatively called the bile duct) into your small intestine after you've eaten a meal. Here, it acts a bit like a detergent and helps to break down fats so that they can be more easily absorbed.

Unfortunately, some people can develop stones inside their gallbladder, which can cause problems, not to mention a little pain, as it tries to squeeze them out. In this chapter we will look at why you might get these stones, the problems they cause, and how you can be rid of them.

What are gallstones?
As the name suggests, they are hard little lumps that look and feel like stones, which form inside the gallbladder. They can take years to form and they range in size from small bits of gravel to

quite large stones that can almost completely fill the gallbladder. Some people will just have one stone, but it's not unusual to have more, especially if they are quite small.

They form when there is an imbalance in the concentrations of the different chemicals that make up the bile in the gallbladder: bile salts, cholesterol, and calcium. So if you have more cholesterol than bile salts, the cholesterol will solidify to make stones. Likewise, if you have a higher concentration of bile salts and calcium than cholesterol, you will develop stones made of these chemicals.

By far the most common type of stone, accounting for 80 per cent of them, are those made of cholesterol, with stones made of bile salts and calcium coming next. A few people have stones that are a combination of all of these chemicals.

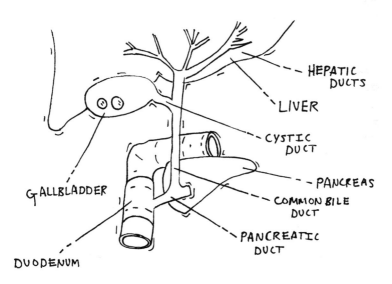

The gallbladder and its neighbouring ducts and organs

Who gets gallstones?

Gallstones have seemingly been around as long as humanity itself. Archaeologists have found 3,000-year-old mummies in Egypt with stones inside their gallbladders. They are most common in people from North America, Europe, and Australasia, and occur less frequently in people from Africa, India, and the Far East. It's thought that around 10–15 per cent of adults will get them at some time.

Mythbuster

Only fat, fair-haired women over 40 get gallstones.

So we were told as medical students. But I've come across patients who have been younger, thinner, and had an olive complexion.

Nevertheless, the textbooks tell us that those who form gallstones most frequently are:

- women (especially those on the contraceptive pill)
- over 40 years old
- obese
- people with a family history of gallstones
- patients with liver cirrhosis.

The reason for their predominance in women is that the female hormone oestrogen has high levels of cholesterol within it, and when it's broken down, much of it ends up in the gallbladder.

What are the symptoms?

Most people who have gallstones are symptom-free and won't know that they have them until they show up on a scan carried out for something else. They will only cause symptoms if the gallbladder tries to squeeze them out through the bile duct, or if an infection called cholecystitis develops around them.

If you do develop symptoms, then these will be:

- Pain, particularly in the upper right-hand side or middle of your abdomen. This pain can be constant, but it is often intermittent and gripping (what's known in the trade as biliary colic pain) and is triggered by eating a meal, particularly a fatty one such as a takeaway. The pain can be severe enough to be mistaken for a stomach ulcer or even a heart attack.

- Nausea and vomiting.

- Sweating.

If you have cholecystitis, then you are likely to experience the following as well:

- a high temperature

- shivering and shaking

- constant severe pain

- yellowing of the skin and whites of the eyes (jaundice)

- diarrhoea

- loss of appetite

- confusion.

How are they diagnosed?
If you have any of the symptoms above, then you will either want to consult your GP or, if the symptoms are severe enough, take a trip to a hospital emergency department. Diagnosis will be made by taking a full medical history of your symptoms and by carefully examining you.

Blood tests may also help to make the diagnosis, particularly tests of liver function, which can be raised when you have gallstones. The test that clinches the diagnosis is usually an ultrasound scan, which is very good at picking up these stones, telling how many there are, and showing whether any of them have already passed and so stretched the bile duct.

How are they treated?

Treatment will depend on whether the stones cause symptoms rather than simply exist in your gallbladder. Stones that cause no symptoms and are found purely by chance are usually left alone, as they may never cause problems. Treating them might carry more risks than benefit. But those that frequently cause colic may need removing.

In the early stages of an attack of colic, symptoms can be managed with strong painkillers at home. If the symptoms don't settle, or an infection is suspected, then hospital admission might be needed for treatment with injectable pain relief and intravenous antibiotics.

Once the acute attack has passed, you may be referred to see a surgeon to consider surgery to take out your gallbladder, a procedure called a cholecystectomy. This not only removes the troublesome stones but, by taking away the gallbladder itself, will stop them reforming. It is usually carried out with keyhole (laparoscopic) surgery if at all possible, although an open operation has to be performed in 5 per cent of cases.

During the surgery, which takes place under general anaesthetic, four small holes about a centimetre long are made in the abdominal wall. Surgeons will insert instruments to help remove the gallbladder through three of these, and a camera will be inserted through the fourth to allow them to view what they are doing on a TV screen in the operating theatre.

Once the gallbladder is cut free, it is usually scooped up in a bag made from the material used for hot air balloons and then removed from the abdomen. The holes are then sealed up and the job is done.

The whole procedure takes up to a couple of hours and, all being well, you will be able to go home the same day, or the next morning at the latest. If you have to have open surgery rather than keyhole, then you will be kept in for a couple of days before discharge, as it's a bigger operation and you will need a bit more time on the ward for recovery. Whichever type of surgery you have, you should be back to normal in around two to three weeks.

Can they be prevented?

Sadly, some of the risk factors for developing gallstones, such as your age and sex, can't be altered. But there's some evidence that a few lifestyle changes might make gallstones less likely:

- Choose a diet that's low in cholesterol.

- Lose weight if you are obese.

- Quit smoking.

- Try exercising for half an hour at least five days per week.

5

Food intolerances

One of the first questions I'm asked when someone either comes to see me about recently acquired bowel symptoms or brings their offspring to discuss tummy ache, frequent runny nappies, or a skin rash is: Do you think this could all be down to a food allergy? And while the answer is invariably no, the question just won't seem to go away.

In fact, it's rare now to go to a restaurant and not see multiple little images, like menu emojis, under each dish to tell diners not only that the meal they're being offered is suitable or unsuitable for vegetarians, but also whether it's free of gluten, fructose, lactose, or whatever other "ose" people can be sensitive to. And then there are dinner parties where you get advance warning that one guest can't eat this food and another might possibly come out in a rash if you feed them that one.

When I was a lad in the good old 1970s, we were happy to eat what we were given, unless it was sprouts. And on the rare occasion we went out to a restaurant for dinner, the menu was pretty much take it or leave it.

So is all this talk of food allergies and intolerances just another modern fad that, like micro-scooters and shoulder pads, will eventually go out of fashion? Or is there something to it that we ignore at our peril?

Is it an allergy or an intolerance?

The first thing we need to get to grips with is the difference between an allergy and an intolerance.

Allergy

An allergy occurs when your immune system identifies a normally harmless substance as a threat to your health and launches an attack against it. This would usually happen when it recognizes a protein molecule on the surface of a potentially infectious bacterium or virus and sets out to destroy it. In an allergic reaction, the response can be so severe that it kills you.

The response triggered by the allergic substance, or allergen, will depend on which part of the body is affected – for example, a rash if it touches your skin or profuse watering if it gets in your eye. But if it's to a food substance that you've swallowed, the reaction can affect your whole body.

Symptoms might include:

- runny nose, sneezing, itchy and watery eyes
- a red, itchy skin rash with hives
- cough, wheeze, and shortness of breath
- abdominal pains, sickness, and diarrhoea.

These symptoms spring up very rapidly after you've been in contact with the allergen, and in severe cases can lead to a condition called anaphylaxis, which can be life-threatening, because it triggers:

- tightness in the throat, with severe breathing difficulties
- dramatic swelling of the face, and hives all over the body
- a sharp drop in blood pressure
- collapse and loss of consciousness.

This sort of allergic reactions can be particularly triggered by:

- nuts
- shellfish
- dairy products
- eggs.

If you are allergic to a particular food, you will be left in no doubt that it is bad for you and you must always avoid it. Your doctor may give you an adrenaline pen (or Epipen) to carry around with you, which you can be trained to self-administer should you develop a sudden reaction.

Intolerance

In contrast to an allergy, a food intolerance is not quite so dramatic and is not life-threatening. But it can nevertheless cause some quite uncomfortable symptoms that can affect the sufferer's day-to-day life and unfortunately may take quite a time to diagnose.

The symptoms of an intolerance can also be wide-ranging, but, unlike with an allergy, these will take hours, rather than minutes, to develop after swallowing whichever food is the main culprit. These symptoms might be:

- headaches
- general lethargy and malaise

- bloating
- abdominal pains and bowel disturbance
- rashes or generalized itching.

Perhaps the two best-known food intolerances are coeliac disease (intolerance to the gluten in wheat) and intolerance to the sugar lactose.

Coeliac disease

Just when you thought you were getting your head around the difference between an allergy and an intolerance, I'm going to throw a spanner in the works because, strictly speaking, coeliac disease isn't actually an intolerance; it's an autoimmune disease.

In autoimmune diseases, which also include conditions such as rheumatoid arthritis and diabetes, the immune system mistakenly attacks normal body tissues instead of invading diseases. And rather than triggering a sudden response as with an allergy, the damage here is done more slowly and usually to an individual organ.

In diabetes, this damage affects production of the hormone insulin from the pancreas gland; in rheumatoid arthritis, it affects the capsules around our joints; and in coeliac disease, it occurs in the walls of the small intestine.

What is coeliac disease?

Coeliac disease is a lifelong autoimmune condition affecting around 1 per cent of the population that is caused by an abnormal reaction to gluten, a mixture of protein molecules found in wheat, barley, and rye. Once ingested, the sufferer's immune system mistakenly identifies the gluten as an invading organism and launches an attack against it.

The fallout from this attack largely affects the walls of the small intestine, which become inflamed. Over time, this inflammation damages the tiny finger-like projections from the walls of the intestine, called villi, which help to absorb nutrients produced during digestion, and this leads to the symptoms of the condition.

Coeliac disease can run in families and it's thought that around 10 per cent of people with the condition will have picked it up as a "family heirloom". Another possible cause is a viral infection of the gut in childhood, but for many people the cause remains unknown.

What are the symptoms?
Most of the symptoms of the condition affect the digestive system and include:

- abdominal pain
- bloating and flatulence
- mouth ulcers
- a change in bowel habit to diarrhoea or constipation.

Non-digestive symptoms include hair loss, weight loss, tiredness, and anaemia.

If left untreated, coeliac disease can cause significant complications, particularly malabsorption of iron, vitamins, and minerals, which can lead to malnutrition and osteoporosis (thinning of the bones). It's therefore important to discover the diagnosis as soon as possible.

How is it diagnosed?
If you think you may have the symptoms of coeliac disease, or if it runs in your family, then you can visit your GP to discuss your

concerns. They may also suggest you are tested for it if you have symptoms of irritable bowel syndrome or develop anaemia.

First, a blood sample will be taken and analysed for the antibodies that are produced in the autoimmune reaction in coeliac disease. If this test is positive, then the next step will be a referral for an endoscopy of the small bowels so that biopsies can be taken. Sometimes, even though the blood test is negative, your doctor may still suggest a referral for a biopsy, particularly if your symptoms are very severe. Once a biopsy is taken, it is examined under the microscope to check for the signs of inflammation and damage to villi that are seen in coeliac disease.

How is it treated?

The key to treating coeliac disease is to avoid eating food containing gluten. Once diagnosed, your gastroenterologist or GP will advise you on the kinds of foods you can and cannot have, and they may also refer you to a dietitian for specific advice. Many large supermarkets now sell specific gluten-free foods and some products may be available on prescription.

As a general guide, the following foods contain gluten and should be avoided unless they are labelled gluten-free:

- bread
- pasta
- cereals
- biscuits
- cakes and pastries
- pizza bases
- pies
- sauces and gravies.

Lactose intolerance

Lactose is a type of sugar found in dairy products. It's reckoned that around 2 per cent of us have an intolerance to this sugar, generally caused by a lack of the enzyme lactase needed to break it down.

What are the symptoms?

The symptoms of lactose intolerance are remarkably similar to those of coeliac disease, with abdominal pains, diarrhoea, wind, and bloating all being features. Motions can also sometimes be a bit foamy.

These symptoms generally begin in the late teenage years and early adulthood, but they can occasionally start in younger and older people. Some people, particularly babies and young children, develop a temporary version of the condition after a bout of gastroenteritis. This tends to resolve itself after a couple of weeks.

How is it diagnosed?

The simplest way to start searching for a cause of your symptoms is by keeping a diet and symptom diary in which you record everything you've had to eat and drink each day for a couple of weeks and make a note alongside of the kinds of symptoms, if any, you've had in your digestive system. You can then take this information with you to your GP when you go to discuss your symptoms.

The next step may also be a bit DIY as your doctor is likely to suggest checking your hunch that dairy products are to blame for your symptoms by stopping eating and drinking them. Once again, a fortnight's trial should be sufficient: if your symptoms have disappeared, you will know that lactose is the likely culprit. If you want to do a final check to confirm things, simply start back on the dairy again and wait for the cramps to kick back in and your poo to turn foamy.

These basic experiments on your digestion are normally all that's needed to make the diagnosis, but if you need more hard-core, scientific tests for lactose intolerance, then your GP may suggest a referral to a gastroenterologist.

The gastroenterologist may suggest one of two tests:

- *A hydrogen breath test.* The hydrogen level in your breath will be analysed before you drink a solution of lactulose, with a repeat level being checked a couple of hours later. If the level of hydrogen goes up, it will confirm the diagnosis of lactose intolerance.

- *A lactose tolerance test.* Here, you will have an initial blood test to measure your baseline level of glucose. Next, you have a drink of lactose solution and a follow-up blood sample will be taken to see what has happened to your glucose level. A rise in glucose suggests lactose is being broken down successfully, whereas no change in the level will demonstrate lactose intolerance.

How is it treated?
The best way to avoid the symptoms of intolerance to lactose is to avoid lactose. It's found in all kinds of dairy products and foods in which they are ingredients, such as:

- milk (from cows, goats, and sheep)
- butter
- cheese
- yoghurt
- cakes and biscuits
- sweets and chocolates
- some salad cream and mayonnaise.

These days many supermarkets have products that are specially made to be lactose-free, and you will find a whole range of different things. You can also try milk and its products from other sources, such as soya, almond, rice, and coconut milks, to name a few.

Medicines can also contain lactose and you'll want to avoid these. Your pharmacist will be able to check whether your pills are lactose-free or not and suggest alternatives for your GP to prescribe.

Finally, you will need to ensure that you make up for the decreased amount of calcium you'll be getting in your diet as a result of ditching the dairy. Other good sources would be green leafy vegetables, soya beans, and nuts. And, of course, you can pick up a bottle of calcium pills to supplement your diet from pharmacies and supermarkets.

Mythbuster

Food allergies and intolerances can be cured.
Unfortunately, there's no cure for any of them: the only way to treat them is to avoid the foods you are sensitive to.

6

Irritable bowel syndrome (IBS) 1: What is it?

Irritable bowel syndrome is the name given to a very common disorder of the digestive system that is estimated to affect around 10–20 per cent of the populations of developed countries. It's a chronic (long-term), recurrent condition which is more common in women than men and can affect people of all ages, including children.

Although it can be quite debilitating at times, it is usually effectively managed by GPs rather than hospital specialists. In this chapter we'll look at the most common symptoms that people with IBS experience, the way it's investigated to rule out more serious bowel pathology, and the treatments that are available to reduce its impact on day-to-day life.

What are the symptoms of IBS?
Not only will the symptoms of IBS vary from person to person, but individual sufferers can also experience different symptom patterns from time to time too. In general, though, the symptoms outlined below will commonly be experienced by most people with the disorder.

Abdominal pain

Pain is often the most troublesome symptom experienced by people with IBS. It usually has the following features:

- It's a cramping type of pain which tends to come and go in spasms (although a few people do have constant pain).
- It can happen anywhere in the abdomen, rather than being in just one particular spot, and it can move around and show up in different places at different times.
- It is often relieved by opening your bowels.
- It may increase at the time when other IBS symptoms get worse.
- It may include a sharp pain low down in the rectum.

Bloating

One of the other common symptoms people notice with IBS is bloating. This tends to increase as the day goes on and can mean that, by the end of the day, clothes that fitted easily in the morning can feel tight. Many of my patients will tell me it makes them feel as if they are pregnant.

Bloating can come on really quickly, often after meals. It tends to get better with lying down, particularly overnight. It is often associated with production of excessive wind.

Change in frequency or consistency of bowel movements

IBS tends to completely mess up your bowel habit. It can cause either constipation or diarrhoea and most often an intermittent mixture of the two.

When constipation is the main problem, you might experience all or some of the following:

- infrequent stools
- needing to strain

- producing small, hard, rabbit-dropping-type motions
- a feeling of incomplete emptying
- wanting to go but having nothing to pass.

At the other end of the toiletry scale, when it's diarrhoea that strikes it can include the following symptoms:

- loose stools
- increased frequency of feeling the need to go
- urgency in getting to a toilet, especially in the mornings (the so-called "morning rush")
- a feeling of having incompletely emptied the bowels
- passage of mucus from the back passage.

Other symptoms
Although the B in IBS stands for bowels, the symptoms it causes can affect far more than just the digestive system. So if you have IBS, you might also have the misfortune of:

- lack of energy and a feeling of being tired all the time
- nausea
- bladder irritability, which can present itself as having to go to the toilet frequently to pass urine both day and night
- backache
- for women, pain during sex
- interrupted sleep, meaning it's not refreshing
- painful periods.

How is IBS diagnosed?
At the moment there is no specific test to help doctors diagnose IBS. Instead, a diagnosis is made based on the presence of

specific symptoms, the absence of other worrying symptoms, and negative results from tests that are able to look for other abdominal conditions.

Medical history

If you see your doctor with abdominal symptoms suggesting IBS, they will want to take a detailed history of when these symptoms began and what does and doesn't make them any easier.

The criteria used by many doctors to diagnose IBS are called the Rome III criteria. The main symptom is recurrent abdominal pain or discomfort at least three days per month in the last three months associated with two or more of the following:

- improvement with defaecation
- change in the frequency of stools
- change in the appearance or form of stools.

The criteria also list other symptoms that cumulatively support the diagnosis of IBS. And alongside those listed above, these include abnormal passage of stool (meaning straining, urgency, or feeling of incomplete emptying) and bloating.

The symptoms that would be concerning to GPs and trigger either further tests (such as a colonoscopy) or referral to a specialist, because they are *not* typical of IBS, are:

- unexplained weight loss
- anaemia
- rectal bleeding
- a change in bowel habit to persistent diarrhoea lasting more than six weeks
- strong family history of bowel or ovarian cancers.

Physical examination

Your doctor will want to carry out a thorough examination of your abdomen to check for any physical signs, again to assess whether there is anything pointing away from IBS. In IBS the abdomen may be non-specifically tender when pressed but is otherwise likely to be normal. If the doctor can feel any masses within the abdomen or lumps in the rectum, then referral for more detailed investigation will need to take place.

Investigation

Once again, these tests will be performed to rule out other diagnoses and won't positively identify IBS itself. The investigations will include simple blood checks for anaemia, inflammation, coeliac disease, and, in women with bloating, ovarian cancer (the CA125 test). A stool sample may also be requested, again to check for inflammation.

If the symptoms meet the criteria above and the blood and stool samples are normal, then a diagnosis of IBS will be made. If, however, your symptoms aren't clear-cut or you have any worrying features, then you may need to go on to have either an abdominal scan or a colonoscopy, or a direct referral to a gastroenterologist.

Treatment

Thankfully, given the troubling nature of the symptoms of IBS for many people, there are a whole range of treatments available to help it. These include not only pills on prescription, but also dietary changes and some complementary therapies. We'll look at them all in a bit more detail in the next chapter.

7

Irritable bowel syndrome (IBS) 2: How is it treated?

As we saw in the last chapter, because IBS is a syndrome rather than a disease, it can manifest itself in different ways, with different people potentially having different clusters of symptoms. Because of this variation in the condition itself, it will come as no surprise that there isn't a one-size-fits-all treatment for it either. One person's miracle cure may even make another person's symptoms much worse, although that happens very rarely.

The treatments covered in this chapter are those for which there is evidence to suggest that they will help most people. Of course, you might well be the odd one out, but do persevere because there will be a treatment out there that suits you and makes the life of your bowels a lot easier to cope with.

Simple dietary advice

One of the first things your doctor, or dietician if you are referred to one (ask your GP), will ask about is which foods you've found make your symptoms worse or better. In some cases, it might be that by simply avoiding things that make your condition worse and eating those that either help or create no problems at all, you can make your IBS better on your own.

This can prove problematic, as it did for the chap I see whose symptoms are made worse by his favourite food: chocolate. As a result, he's had to curb his chocoholic cravings most of the time, but he does allow himself the odd treat, knowing that 12 hours later it won't be a treat for his tummy.

It's not always obvious what your personal IBS triggers are food-wise, so it's often a good idea to keep a food diary every day for a few weeks to see if anything you eat has an obvious, repeated link to bringing on symptoms. This diary can be as simple or as detailed as you like. It can either just focus on the food you eat and when you eat it each day or include other details such as whether you were stressed that day and even the colour and consistency of your poo.

You can use an ordinary diary or notebook to record your findings, but lots of IBS-related and general health organizations have ready-made diary sheets you can download to help you. Just type "IBS food diary" into your internet search engine and plenty of options will pop up.

Alongside your own specific dietary dos and don'ts, there is also a lot of general advice around for all IBS sufferers when it comes to meal times:

- Have regular meals and try not to skip any or have long gaps between meal times.

- Take your time over eating and don't wolf food down as if someone's going to take it away from you if you don't.

- Cut down on caffeinated and fizzy drinks such as tea, coffee, and cola.

- Drink plenty of water every day (the recommended intake is around 1.5 to 2 litres each day).

- Cook from fresh when possible and avoid processed and takeaway foods and fat-laden snacks such as crisps, cakes, and biscuits.

- Only eat three, rather than the generally recommended five, portions of fruit and vegetables each day.

- If you suffer with a lot of wind and bloating, cut down on beans, pulses, and Brussels sprouts.

Fibre

The amount of fibre in your diet can play a part in the extent to which you experience symptoms of IBS. Fibre comes in two forms: soluble and insoluble. Sources of soluble fibre, which dissolves in water and ferments in the bowel, include oats, barley, fruit, and root vegetables, whereas insoluble fibre is found in cereals, nuts, and wholemeal bread.

Fibre is thought to help regulate bowel habits and improve the symptoms of IBS in most people with the condition, but it's most helpful if you find constipation particularly troubling. If that's you, then it's recommended that you increase the amount of soluble and insoluble fibre that you eat. It's best to do this slowly to help your gut get used to it gradually and not generate too much gas along the way.

Low FODMAP diet

FODMAP stands for: fermentable oligosaccharides, disaccharides, monosaccharides, and polyols (hence the much shorter and snappier acronym used to describe it). These different saccharides and polyols are types of carbohydrate that ferment inside the bowel.

Cutting down on foods containing these FODMAPs can reduce many of the more troublesome symptoms of IBS, such as bloating, abdominal pain, wind, and alterations in bowel habit. And it's worth giving it a go because it's reckoned to help at least 70 per cent of people with IBS who try it.

Having said all that, it's quite a complicated diet to follow accurately, and although there are many FODMAP diet sheets you can download from the internet to try to follow, your doctor may suggest that you see a dietician before starting so that they can go through things with you and give you a proper diet plan. By all means check out some of the resources that are available online, but if you're serious about trying this diet, it's best to see your GP first.

Probiotics

These are bacteria or yeasts that are thought to have health benefits. They are added to drinks, yoghurts, and supplements, and are often described in TV adverts as "good" bacteria.

It's thought that they can help symptoms of IBS by restoring the balance of natural bacteria within the bowel which can be disturbed by infections and certain medicines. The evidence for this is quite sparse, but most experts suggest they are worth a go.

The advice is to give one form of probiotic a try for around four weeks, and if your IBS is not helped by then, try switching to another. These products are available in all major supermarkets, so are pretty easy to get hold of, and the worst they will do is nothing.

Alternative therapies

Many of the most commonly available alternative therapies are touted as treatments for IBS, and I've had patients who have been helped by visiting a homeopath, having acupuncture and reflexology, undergoing hypnosis, and swallowing herbal remedies such as those containing peppermint.

They don't help everyone and unfortunately there's precious little scientific evidence to advise their use. But if they are safe for you to try, there's no harm in having a go.

Drug treatments

The drugs available for treatment of your IBS are:

- laxatives
- antispasmodics
- anti-motility agents
- anti-foaming agents
- antidepressants
- linaclotides

In this section we will take a quick look at these drugs to see how they work and what symptoms they aim to treat.

Laxatives

There are different types of drugs in this category which have been designed to help clear constipation. They do this in one of three ways: by making stools softer (as in the case of the medicine lactulose), by stimulating the wall of the bowel to squeeze things through more quickly (which is what tablets containing senna do), or by making stools bulkier so that they can pass more easily.

The most useful laxatives used in IBS are those in this last group, which make the stools bulkier. An example from this group is ispaghula which is found in the proprietary brand Fybogel. The others, lactulose and senna, which can be bought over the counter from the pharmacy, are best avoided, as they can make things worse.

Antispasmodics

These drugs relax the smooth muscle in the wall of the intestine and so help prevent the painful spasms that can be such an annoying and uncomfortable feature of IBS. The choices available include: hyoscine (Buscopan), mebeverine (Colofac), and peppermint oil (Colpermin).

Anti-motility agents

This group of medicines work by slowing down the muscular contractions in the wall of the intestine which cause the developing faeces to move down through the bowels towards their exit. As a result of the increased transit time, more water can be absorbed from inside the bowels into the bloodstream, making the stools firmer.

The most commonly prescribed drug in this group is loperamide (Imodium). It can also be bought directly from your pharmacist.

Anti-foaming agents

These drugs, of which simethicone (Wind-eze) is the most commonly used, join up small gas bubbles within the digestive tract into bigger ones so that they can be passed (farted) more easily. They are used to relieve the pain and discomfort from bloating in IBS by helping to remove the cause.

Antidepressants

Two groups of antidepressant drugs are used in treating symptoms in IBS: tricyclic antidepressants (TCAs) and selective serotonin reuptake inhibitors (thankfully shortened to SSRIs). They are not being used for their antidepressant properties but because they can reduce the intensity of pain signals travelling through nerves from the gut to the brain.

TCAs are usually tried first, but if they don't work, or they cause constipation, which is one of their possible side effects, you may be offered an SSRI instead. However, if you are suffering with symptoms of anxiety that are making your IBS worse, then you may be tried on SSRIs from the start, as they are effective in relieving symptoms of anxiety as well.

Linaclotide

This is a new drug which has a number of actions that help to reduce symptoms in IBS. It works first by reducing pain from the bowel muscle wall, and then it improves the passage of faeces through the gut both by increasing the fluid within the bowel to soften them and by increasing the rate at which they then move through it.

Which of these drugs or groups of drugs your doctor will recommend that you try will depend on what your predominant symptoms are. To help with this choice, IBS is often classified into three main types:

- IBS-C where constipation is the main bowel symptom
- IBS-D where it's diarrhoea that causes most trouble
- IBS-M where people's symptoms fluctuate between constipation and diarrhoea.

The recommended treatments for each are shown in the table below, with linaclotide and the antidepressants being added into your medication list if the other medicines don't help.

IBS-C	IBS-D	IBS-M
Laxatives	Anti-motility agent	Antispasmodics
Antispasmodics	Antispasmodics	Anti-foaming agents
Anti-foaming agents	Anti-foaming agents	Anti-foaming agents
Linaclotide	TCA	SSRIs

Psychological therapies

If you are unfortunate enough to have stubborn symptoms that you just can't shake off despite trying the treatments we've discussed, your doctor might suggest that you be referred for some psychological therapy. These therapies, which can include counselling, cognitive behavioural therapy (CBT), and hypnotherapy, can help provide you with strategies both to reduce the impact that your IBS has on you and to help deal with any life stresses that might be triggering or exaggerating your symptoms.

For more information on psychotherapy and how it works, check out the useful resources in the appendix.

Future treatment

Given time, there will no doubt be more drugs on the market to tackle the symptoms of IBS. But recently an altogether different treatment, which is already helping people with the particularly nasty gut infection called *Clostridium difficile* ("C diff" for short), has been touted by researchers as a potential new therapy for IBS as well: faecal transplants.

I'll be honest with you, when I first heard about these transplants, I thought that either the patient who was telling me about them was having me on or they were some whacky alternative therapy that sensible clinicians wouldn't touch with a bargepole. But having read a paper published in the esteemed *New England Journal of Medicine*, I have been enlightened, although I'm still not sure I'd fancy having one myself.

The process involves collecting a sample of faeces from a healthy donor, which, after undergoing treatment, is placed into the bowel of a recipient, either by endoscopy or using an enema. The transplanted faeces then increase the levels of good bacteria in the bowel, re-establishing a healthy balance and putting bad bacteria back in their place.

It's a bit like having a whopping dose of the probiotics we discussed earlier, although thankfully here you don't have to drink the sample. It's still in its infancy as a treatment for IBS, but early research has shown very positive results. So watch this space.

8

Diverticular disease

This digestive condition, which is specific to the large intestine, is thought to affect the bowels of about half of the population of the world's most developed countries. It's particularly prevalent in Western Europe and North America and becomes more common as we get older, with an estimated 70 per cent of us who make it to the age of 80 developing it.

In this chapter we'll take a look at what the condition is, the problems it can lead to, and the ways in which its effects can be minimized. Thankfully, despite its near ubiquitous presence in the bowels of the over-50s, many of us will never be made aware that it's there.

What is diverticular disease?

"Diverticulum", a word derived from Latin, is used in medical parlance to describe a little pouch. The pouches in question are formed when the lining of the large bowel pushes out through small gaps in the surrounding muscle wall. From the outside this gives it the appearance of bubble wrap, but the bubbles aren't quite so poppable and they are also spread further apart than they are in the plastic wrapping material. Each "bubble" on the outside corresponds to a pouch inside.

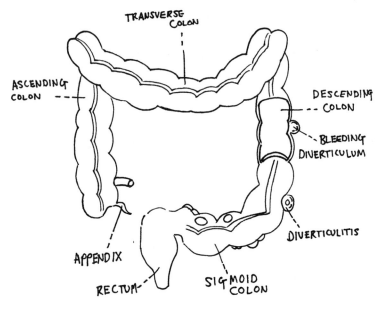

The large bowel with some diverticulae

The pouches themselves don't always cause people any bother – in fact, only about 20 per cent of people with them will develop symptoms – but if a small lump of faeces becomes trapped in one and starts to fester, then the gut bacteria it contains can multiply and cause an infection. The pouch then becomes inflamed, producing what's then called diverticulitis.

What causes diverticular disease?
No one is 100 per cent sure about the cause of diverticular disease, but all the available evidence points towards a lack

of fibre in people's diet as being the main culprit. A second aggravating cause is believed to be the Western habit of sitting down to have a poo. Both of these factors lead to increased pressure inside the bowel which forces the inner lining out through the muscle wall, creating the diverticulae. Once formed, these pouches never return to their original position.

In contrast, a diet that's rich in indigestible fibre from food sources such as nuts, jacket potatoes, brown rice, wholegrain bread, and most fruit and vegetables helps keep stools bulkier, which means that they pass more easily and so keep the pressure inside the bowel low. And the squatting position, adopted by people in many developing countries to empty their bowels, keeps the large intestine straighter inside the body, which again makes the exit of waste products quicker and easier than when sitting down.

It's perhaps no surprise, then, that rates of diverticular disease are much lower in countries where people have a more natural diet and only the most basic lavatorial facilities. Those of us who use a plumbed-in toilet rather than a drop hole outside can replicate the squatting position by putting our feet on a foot stool while we sit on the loo, which can apparently make evacuation less of a strain.

What are the symptoms?
As we've seen already, many people with diverticular disease get away without suffering from any symptoms at all. Those who aren't quite so lucky will experience different symptoms depending on whether they are simply due to having diverticulae in their bowels or whether they are having a bout of diverticulitis.

Symptoms of diverticular disease

People can experience some or all of the following:

- Intermittent bouts of lower left-hand-sided abdominal pain. This pain can be worse during or just after mealtimes and can be relieved by going to the toilet or simply passing wind (which perhaps ought to be saved until after you've left the dinner table).

- An alteration in bowel habit from its usual pattern to either looser bowels or full-on diarrhoea, or constipation.

- Abdominal bloating.

- Rectal bleeding, with dark red blood from the back passage.

Symptoms of diverticulitis

These symptoms are far more severe and include:

- Left lower-abdominal pain. This might come and go but will generally be far more intense than the pain of diverticular disease itself.

- Fever.

- Nausea, vomiting, and lost appetite.

- Change in bowel habit. This is most often to looser bowels with perhaps full-on diarrhoea, but I have known people whose bowels have gone the other way and their infection has triggered constipation.

In extreme or repeated cases of diverticulitis, there's a risk of developing some potentially serious complications such as bowel perforation, abscesses around the bowel, heavy rectal bleeding, and even bowel obstruction. For this reason it's important to seek medical attention quickly if you have any of the symptoms of diverticulitis listed above.

How is it diagnosed?

If your doctor thinks that your symptoms are suggestive of diverticular disease, then it's likely that they will send you for either a colonoscopy or virtual colonoscopy (see Chapter 2). It's also very common to have it picked up coincidentally when you're having a bowel test looking for something else.

If you are already known to have diverticular disease and your doctor is wondering if your symptoms are due to diverticulitis, they might send you for some blood tests looking for signs of inflammation and infection.

How can it be treated?

For the many people who develop diverticular disease but are lucky enough never to be bothered by symptoms, no treatment is strictly necessary. But given that it is triggered by increased pressure in the bowel brought on by a low-fibre diet, increasing the amount of dietary fibre is likely to help things remain symptom-free and prevent the condition from getting worse.

For those who do have symptoms, advice about eating more fruit, vegetables, nuts, and beans to raise the fibre content of the diet is important to follow, as this will minimize flare-ups of the symptoms and stop the condition becoming worse. But dietary alterations alone might not be enough to improve things. If you are in this category, your doctor will be able to prescribe some high-fibre medicines that will help not only improve symptoms but also keep you regular.

Pain should really only be treated with paracetamol because drugs such as codeine and ibuprofen can actually make things worse. If you are in doubt about what to try, or your pain is particularly severe, then, again, seek advice from your doctor.

A bout of diverticulitis will almost certainly warrant a trip to your GP to help settle it down. It is usually treated with oral antibiotics, which should resolve things after a week's course. Your doctor will also advise you to drink plenty of fluids to avoid dehydration.

If your symptoms are severe, if oral antibiotics don't help, or if you are vomiting and can't take medicines by mouth, you may need admission to a hospital surgical ward. This doesn't mean you'll have to have an operation, but you'll end up there because surgeons are the specialists who tend to treat diverticulitis.

Treatment on the ward will involve intravenous antibiotics and fluids (a drip), but it can mean an operation if you develop any of the serious complications listed above, such as obstruction, an abscess, or bowel perforation.

Can it be prevented?

As we've already seen, the best way to prevent diverticular disease developing is to enjoy a diet crammed full of fibre. This means getting those all-important five portions of fruit and vegetables every day and adding in foods such as wholemeal bread, brown rice, oats, lentils, beans, dried fruit, and high-fibre breakfast cereal.

If you really want to avoid it, then you can also follow the example of people in developing countries by squatting to go to the toilet! But a daily dose of fibre should be a helpful start if you don't fancy making a change in your toilet posture.

9

Inflammatory bowel disease

There are two conditions that are classified as inflammatory bowel diseases: Crohn's disease and ulcerative colitis. They affect around 300,000 people in the UK, 2.5 million people across Europe in total, and a further 1 million people in the United States.

Although they produce similar symptoms, there are some crucial differences between these two disorders. In this chapter we will take a look at each in turn.

Crohn's disease

Crohn's disease is named after an American gastroenterologist called Burrill Crohn who, although not the first physician to identify the condition, was the one who published most cases and established its place in the medical textbooks. It's a lifelong disease that can cause inflammation throughout the length of the bowel from the mouth to the anus, but tends to crop up most frequently in the ileum and colon.

What causes it?

There doesn't seem to be one single cause for the condition and it's thought that it develops because of a combination of different factors all ganging up on someone together. These include:

- *Genetics*. Crohn's disease can run in families, and if you have a twin with the condition, you have a 70 per cent chance of developing it yourself. Researchers have also discovered a number of genes that are more commonly found in people who have Crohn's than in those who don't.

- *Faulty immune response*. There's evidence that the immune system in people with Crohn's has a slight malfunction. It sees the good bacteria in the gut as invading organisms and so attacks them. This causes inflammation in the bowel wall.

- *Cigarettes*. Smokers are twice as likely to develop Crohn's than non-smokers and their symptoms are also likely to be worse than those of people with Crohn's who don't smoke.

- *Environmental factors*. The place where you live seems to have an impact on your likelihood of developing the disease. It is far more common in city dwellers and those living in developed countries where poor diet is believed to play a part.

What are the symptoms?

Symptoms can develop at any time of life but usually appear between the ages of 10 and 40. In many people the symptoms come on gradually, although they can appear all of a sudden for some. They are not constant, though, and Crohn's sufferers will often experience long periods of time when they are symptom-free.

The types of symptoms that crop up will depend on which part of the gut is affected by the disease. As we've seen, this is usually the bottom end of the ileum and the colon. The possible symptoms are:

- abdominal pain and diarrhoea, which often has blood in it
- extreme fatigue
- feverishness
- loss of appetite
- mouth ulcers
- red lumps on the skin, particularly on the legs
- unexplained weight loss
- inflammation of the eyes (uveitis)
- joint pain and swelling.

How is it diagnosed?

It would be very surprising if anyone who developed these symptoms didn't immediately book an appointment to see their doctor as they can be quite severe and often debilitating; they certainly aren't the kind of symptoms that can be ignored.

Your GP will follow the usual protocol of first taking a medical history, then carrying out a physical examination, and finally arranging for you to have some tests. The kind of investigations they will arrange for you are:

- Blood tests looking for signs of inflammation, infection, or anaemia, and to check for normal liver and kidney function.
- Stool samples will be sent to look for signs of infection, and they can also be tested for inflammation by looking for a raised level of a protein called calprotectin: the higher the calprotectin level, the more inflamed the bowels are.

- An endoscopy may also be requested, particularly a colonoscopy, a sigmoidoscopy, or a capsule endoscopy. Not only will this allow doctors to get a good look at the bowel wall with the almost naked eye, but it will also give them a chance to take biopsies, which can then be sent to the lab and examined under the microscope for the tell-tale signs of Crohn's.

- Scans, such as CT and MRI scans, can help specialists look at the extent of the disease once picked up.

For more detail on these tests, please take a look back at Chapter 2.

How is it treated?

The type of treatment used will depend on the extent of the disease within the bowel, how severe the symptoms are, and whether or not any complications have developed. Some people can be treated as outpatients, with input from their family doctor, while others may need immediate admission to hospital and even have to go under a surgeon's knife if things are bad enough.

The medicines used to manage Crohn's are unlikely to be started by your GP unless they have spoken to a gastroenterologist first. Most will be initiated in hospital by your specialist team, with instructions about how long to continue them, how to reduce the dose, and any monitoring that's needed (perhaps with regular blood tests) passed on to your GP so that they can help support you at home.

Unfortunately, there isn't yet a cure for Crohn's disease, and the drugs prescribed are used first to reduce symptoms and bring on a remission of the disease, and second to maintain that remission. Medicines used to induce remission might include:

- *Corticosteroid drugs such as prednisolone and hydrocortisone.* Both of these can reduce inflammation in the bowel, but they can rapidly cause unwanted side effects, such as weight gain, thinning of the bones, and increased susceptibility to infections. As a result, once they've done their job, the dose is tapered off and they are stopped. They come in many forms and can be given as pills, injections, and even foams and suppositories which go directly up your bottom.

- *5-aminosalicylates such as mesalazine.* These drugs also reduce inflammation and have fewer side effects than steroids, but many people don't find them as effective at calming their Crohn's down.

When it comes to maintaining remission, the simplest treatment is to stop smoking if you are a smoker. You may also opt just to wait and see what happens and take no further treatment unless you have another flare-up. But if you have frequent flare-ups, there are a couple of types of drug you might be advised to try:

- *Immunosuppressants such as azathioprine and methotrexate.* These medicines also reduce inflammation, this time by targeting the immune system in order to stop it producing the chemicals that cause the inflammation in the first place. Though often effective, they aren't without their side effects, which can be too much for some people (e.g. nausea and vomiting, inflammation of the pancreas, increased likelihood of picking up infections). They also need monitoring with frequent blood tests.

- *TNF inhibitors, including infliximab and adalimumab.* These drugs are used to treat severe disease. They target a specific protein that causes infection in Crohn's called tumour necrosis factor (TNF). They are given in hospital as injections and need close follow-up by specialists during the 12 months or so that you will be given them.

For some people, though, surgery may be needed, particularly when they develop some of the more severe complications of Crohn's:

- Fistulas, which are small channels that can run from your bowels to other parts of your body such as your anus, bladder, or vagina. These fistulas can lead to some pretty awful infections in very unwanted places.
- Strictures, where inflammation of the walls inside the bowel causes scar tissue to develop, resulting in narrowing of the diameter of the bowel itself and possible obstruction.
- Abscesses, when infections in the bowel cause collections of pus to form.

Finally, surgery might be needed to remove stretches of the bowel that are particularly inflamed and troublesome, and where symptoms don't settle down, whatever medical treatments are tried.

Ulcerative colitis
This is the other inflammatory bowel disease which, like Crohn's disease, is a lifelong illness. Unlike Crohn's, however, it doesn't affect the whole bowel but, as its name suggests, is confined to the colon.

What causes it?
As with Crohn's disease, there doesn't seem to be one specific cause for ulcerative colitis. It seems to be triggered by a combination of factors, including genetics (it runs in families),

 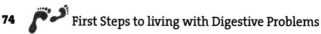

abnormalities in the way the immune system responds to bacterial infections, smoking, and other environmental factors (like Crohn's, it is more commonly seen in cities in developed countries).

What are the symptoms?
Again, like Crohn's disease, it can develop at any time in life, but the symptoms most commonly show up in younger people from the ages of 15 to 25. These symptoms are also pretty similar and include:

- diarrhoea, often mixed with blood
- abdominal pain
- needing to empty your bowels many times each day (10–20 times for some poor people)
- loss of appetite
- weight loss
- fever
- anaemia
- arthritis
- mouth ulcers.

How is it diagnosed?
With symptoms so similar to Crohn's disease, it's perhaps no surprise that the investigations will be similar too. Your doctor may have a hunch from the history they take from you that you have ulcerative colitis rather than Crohn's because of your family history. But they will still want to perform the same examination and carry out the same blood and stool tests.

It's likely that the diagnosis will be clinched by the results of biopsies and changes in the bowel wall visualized at endoscopy which highlight the differences between the two diseases. As we've seen, whereas the changes in Crohn's disease are seen throughout the bowel, in ulcerative colitis they will only be seen in the colon and the lower part of the bowel, particularly the rectum. The lining of the bowel wall in Crohn's disease also has the appearance of cobblestones on its surface, but this isn't the case in ulcerative colitis.

How is it treated?

Having noted some diagnostic differences between the two conditions, we return to similar territory where treatment is concerned. Once more it's about achieving remission and then maintaining it. And the armoury of drugs for ulcerative colitis includes our familiar friends: corticosteroids, 5-aminosalicylates, immunosuppressants, and TNF inhibitors.

The big difference between treatments for Crohn's and ulcerative colitis comes when we consider surgery. Although procedures for Crohn's disease are only able to deal with complications and remove troublesome sections of bowel, in ulcerative colitis surgery can offer a potential cure.

By removing the whole colon, a surgeon can remove the entire cause of the problem. Following what's called an ileo-anal pouch – where the end of the small bowel is made into a pouch and joined to the anus to let motions be stored and then pass normally once the colon is removed – many people can be free from the condition. Of course, the risks of surgery must be considered, so it's not a miracle cure.

10

Cancers of the digestive system

I've written this chapter not to frighten you out of your wits – so that you see cancer in every episode of indigestion, belly ache, or loose bowel motion – but in order that you might be able to recognize the warning signs of potentially serious conditions. That way, you can get to the doctor as soon as possible and have things checked out. It's also aimed at providing a warning about risk factors for the development of these tumours so that you have an even better chance of avoiding them in the first place.

Cancers are, thankfully, rare causes of digestive symptoms, but they are obviously the most serious and they can affect any part of the gut, from top to bottom. So we will once again follow a route from mouth to anus, pointing out the red-flag symptoms that should have you booking in to see your GP.

Mouth
Cancers can crop up on any of the tissues inside the mouth and throat. These include:

- lips
- tongue
- gums
- tonsils
- salivary glands.

Warning signs
Keep an eye out for any persistent symptoms which stick around for more than three weeks. In particular, these should include the following:

- unexplained ulcers or lumps
- a persistent sore or painful throat
- hoarseness of the throat
- difficulty swallowing
- unexplained red or red-and-white patches that are particularly sore or bleeding
- unexplained loose teeth or any other unusual symptoms in the mouth
- new lumps in the neck that don't settle.

You could see your doctor or dentist about these problems. They will be able to assess what's going on and make the appropriate referrals to investigate, or treat and reassure.

Risk factors
You will notice a pattern developing as we look at the risk factors for each set of cancers. But please don't let familiarity breed contempt. If a risk factor keeps cropping up, it should be taken particularly seriously. So the risk factors for cancers of the mouth include:

- smoking
- heavy alcohol consumption
- chewing tobacco
- betel nuts, often chewed by people of South Asian, particularly Indian and Sri Lankan, origin
- oral sex with someone infected with the human papillomavirus (HPV)
- poor dental hygiene.

If you need help with quitting tobacco and alcohol, or advice about sexual health, do see your GP. It's also highly recommended that you are registered with a dentist and attend check-ups every six months.

Oesophageal cancer

Cancer can occur in any part of the oesophagus where it develops in both the cells lining it or the glands that produce secretions onto its surface. It is the thirteenth most common cancer in adults in the UK.

Warning signs

- Difficulty swallowing: food feels as if it's sticking, there's a persistent lump, or you have regurgitation of food.
- Persistent heartburn (burning pain behind the breastbone).
- Weight loss.

If these symptoms persist, certainly for three weeks or more, do see your doctor. They don't mean you have cancer, but your GP will want to be sure you don't.

Risk factors

- Obesity.
- Smoking and chewing tobacco.
- Heavy alcohol consumption.
- Not getting enough fruit and veg in your diet.
- Uncontrolled reflux and indigestion.

Stomach cancer

While not a common cancer, there are around 7,000 people diagnosed with this condition each year in the UK and around 1 million worldwide. People living in the Far East and Central America have the highest incidence of stomach cancers.

Warning signs

- Swallowing difficulties.
- Progressive unintentional weight loss.
- Persistent vomiting.
- Iron-deficiency anaemia.
- A persistent lump or swelling at the top of your abdomen.
- Unexplained worsening of indigestion or upper abdominal pain.
- Passing black stools.

Risk factors

- Smoking.
- Untreated *Helicobacter* infection.
- A diet with poor intake of fruit and vegetables.
- Family history.

 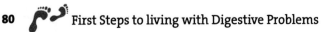

As before, concerns about symptoms or family history of stomach cancer should be discussed with your doctor. Your doctor can also help you quit smoking.

The liver and pancreas

In developed countries, it's rare to develop a cancer in the liver itself, but it is a common site for tumours from other organs to spread to. Rare cancers can also crop up in the gallbladder and bile ducts, and you can develop cancer in the pancreas too.

Warning signs

- An upper abdominal lump or swelling.
- Persistent pain in the centre or upper right of the abdomen.
- The skin turning yellow (jaundiced).

Risk factors

- Smoking.
- Obesity.
- Family history.
- Liver cirrhosis.
- Type 2 diabetes.

These cancers are notorious for only developing symptoms once they are well established and treatment will be difficult. So you must see your doctor immediately if you notice any of the symptoms above and, just as importantly, do what you can to get help to reduce your risk factors where possible.

Smoking

It's well known that smoking can give you lung cancer and chronic chest diseases, as well as put you in the firing line for heart attacks and strokes. But it is also one of the major risk factors for developing cancer elsewhere in the body, especially in the digestive system.

Quitting smoking can be hard, but it's not impossible, and the withdrawal symptoms and cravings it puts you through have got to be worth it when you consider these life-threatening alternatives.

Your family doctor and practice nurse can give you help and support in breaking the habit, and there's loads of helpful advice in another book in the First Steps series: *First Steps out of Smoking*.

Small bowel cancers

Cancers in this part of the digestive system are rare, with around 1,000 new cases each year in the UK. They can occur in the cells lining the small intestine, in the muscle in its walls, in hormone-producing cells along its length, and in the lymph nodes that surround it.

Warning signs
These can be vague, but include:

- dark stools
- persistent abdominal pains
- diarrhoea
- weight loss
- anaemia.

Risk factors

Here, the most common risks come from other conditions you might have affecting your intestines, such as:

- Crohn's disease
- coeliac disease
- family history of polyps.

Large bowel cancers

Cancer of the colon is the fourth most common cancer and it's reckoned that around 1 in 20 people in the UK will develop it at some point in their lifetime. Worldwide, there are around 1.5 million new cases each year.

Warning signs

- A change in bowel habit to looser stools that carries on for six weeks with or without bleeding.
- Rectal bleeding with no piles or other anal symptoms.
- Anaemia.
- A lump in the lower abdomen, rectum, or anus.

Risk factors

- A diet that's low in fibre and fruit and veg, and high in red meat.
- High consumption of alcohol.
- Smoking.
- Obesity.
- Lack of exercise.

In the UK there is a national bowel cancer screening programme which checks men and women between the ages of 60 and 74 (as they are in the highest risk category) for cancer using a simple test for blood in the stool that is repeated every two years. It is well worth taking part.

Mythbuster

Colorectal cancer is always fatal.

If caught early, this type of cancer is 90 per cent curable, which is why it's important to take the screening tests if you are offered them, even if you don't have symptoms.

11

A sore bottom

When it comes to embarrassment about digestion and the bowels, nothing causes people to blush, stutter, or completely clam up more than when they have to come to see me and discuss a problem involving their anus. Not only is it one of the most personal and private parts of the body, but it's also the hole where poo comes from, and no matter how thorough someone's personal hygiene is, it can still feel a bit dirty down there, and the consultation is frequently peppered with unnecessary apologies for having brought this part of their anatomy to my attention.

But as we've seen with any symptoms affecting the bowels, it is not embarrassing for the doctor and it is much better to be safe than sorry. I have a very sad recent memory of a patient who avoided booking an appointment because they didn't want to discuss their ongoing anal symptoms and had convinced themselves it was simply piles and therefore nothing to worry about.

Tragically, it wasn't piles; it was cancer. And by the time I saw this patient, it was beyond treatment.

If you have any symptoms around your bottom, please don't be shy; just get them checked out. They are much more likely to be due to something simple rather than anything rare and life-threatening. But if they are potentially serious, the quicker they are treated the better.

In this chapter we will look at some of the most common problems.

Piles (haemorrhoids)

Piles are probably the most well-known problem that can affect the anus. They are pretty common, with most studies suggesting that around 50 per cent of us will be lucky enough to have them at some point in our life. They generally affect adults and are most likely to crop up between the ages of 45 and 65.

What are haemorrhoids?

Just inside the anus are three anal cushions. These are basically large, engorged veins which are held in place by connective tissues at the lower end of the rectum. They are there to help the sphincter muscle of the anus keep faeces inside us until we are ready to get rid of them when we sit on a toilet.

These cushions become piles when they prolapse through the anus and appear as lumps on the outside: sometimes nicknamed the Grapes of Wrath, because of both their shape and their potential to become painful. They are classified as either first, second, or third degree, depending on how prominent they are:

- First degree will pop in and out on their own after going to the toilet.

- Second degree need to be pushed back by hand.

- Third degree stay outside all the time, no matter what you try and do to them yourself.

What causes them?
The factors that increase your chances of developing piles are:

- prolonged constipation
- frequent diarrhoea
- straining to go to the toilet
- being obese
- lots of heavy lifting
- being pregnant (as a result of the increased pressure inside your abdomen because of your growing baby)
- family history.

Mythbuster

You can get piles by sitting on cold floors.
Contrary to the old wives' tale, there's absolutely no link between the temperature of what you're sitting on and the development of piles. But if you repeatedly strain to go to the toilet when you're sitting on that, then you may well develop some.

What symptoms do they cause?
Piles don't always cause problems, particularly if they are the first-degree "now you see them, now you don't" variety, which may appear and disappear completely unnoticed. If you do get symptoms, they are likely to be one or more of the following:

- Bleeding when you go to the toilet. This is usually bright red and may be either on the toilet paper when you wipe yourself, in the water down the pan, or on the surface of your motions.
- A lump around your anus that might come and go.
- A mucus discharge after going to the toilet.

- Itching and soreness.
- Occasionally pain when passing a motion.

What can be done about them?
Treatments range from lifestyle changes all the way up to surgery:

- *Self-care.* Have plenty of fruit and fibre in your diet and keep well hydrated to avoid constipation and straining. Try to lose weight if you are obese.

- *From the pharmacy.* Simple laxatives such as lactulose will keep your motions soft, and painkillers such as paracetamol will help with the discomfort. There are a variety of soothing creams that your pharmacist can recommend for you too.

- *The GP.* If the suggestions above haven't helped, your GP may prescribe either creams or suppositories (tablets that go up your bottom) containing local anaesthetics and steroids to help the pain and swelling. They may take one look and refer you straight to a specialist.

- *Hospital.* There are treatments available as an outpatient, such as banding (where elastic bands are placed over the piles to cut off the blood supply) and sclerotherapy (when the piles are injected with a chemical that makes them shrivel up). If all else fails, then an operation called a haemorrhoidectomy can be performed.

Anal fissure

What is an anal fissure?
An anal fissure is a small tear or ulcer in the skin around the anus, which is, I'm told, as painful as it sounds. When it comes to causes of a sore bottom, this condition is the Daddy.

Fissures are usually about a centimetre long and a couple of millimetres deep. They tend to occur centrally and at the back of the anus rather than the front.

What causes them?
They are usually caused by trauma to the anal skin either from passing a hard, hefty stool when you are constipated or from recurrent wiping of your bottom during an episode of diarrhoea.

What symptoms do they cause?
The skin around the anus is exceptionally sensitive and so the most prominent symptom of a fissure is pain when going to the toilet. It can be rather severe and different patients have described it to me as being like "pooing glass" or "passing a lump of barbed wire".

Fissures can also cause bleeding when going to the toilet. This, as with piles, is bright red blood and can be seen on either the stool or on the toilet paper.

What can be done about them?
Most settle on their own within a week or two. The healing process can be aided by:

- keeping stools soft by eating plenty of fruit and veg and staying well hydrated
- not "holding on" when you get the urge to go to the toilet
- using soft toilet paper or flushable wet wipes to clean your bottom after passing a motion
- soaking your bottom in the bath to help keep the anal muscle relaxed.

If these simple measures don't work, then your GP may prescribe or recommend some of these treatments:

- a stool softener such as lactulose
- local anaesthetic creams
- GTN or diltiazem ointments, which relax the muscle of the anus and increase blood supply to help healing
- botulinum toxin injections – botox is not just used by the famous and the vain to keep facial wrinkles at bay; it can also stop the anal muscle from going into spasm, which reduces pain and aids healing.

If your fissure is stubborn and still doesn't settle, then you can be referred to a surgeon to consider one of the operations that can help sort them out.

Itchy bottom

We all get a bit of an itch around our bottoms from time to time, but for about 5 per cent of the population it can become a chronic problem which goes by the Latin name of *pruritus ani*.

What causes pruritus ani?

Because the skin of the anus has so many nerve endings, it doesn't take much to make it irritated. This then causes the sensation of itchiness. Scratching will then cause more irritation until an itch–scratch–itch cycle is set up, where the more you itch, the more you scratch and the itchier it becomes and so on.

What causes it?

There are many causes of an itchy bottom:

- being too fastidious about cleanliness and washing with soap too often or rubbing too hard when wiping with toilet paper

- moisture from sweat, vaginal discharge, soiling or mucus around the anus, or nylon underpants

- scented soap or loo paper, or sensitivity to washing powders and shower gels

- skin problems, including dermatitis, fungal infections, and warts

- piles and anal fissures.

Can it be treated?

Most treatment advice is very simple and doesn't involve the use of any medicines or operations. The itch can be reduced by trying the following:

- Keep your bottom clean with daily baths or showers and then dry gently by patting rather than rubbing with a towel.

- Avoid scented soaps.

- Use soft toilet paper or flushable wet wipes after opening your bowels and maybe even bath or shower or use a bidet if you have one.

- Wear cotton underpants.

- Try not to scratch.

Appendix: Useful resources

The information in this book has been gathered from a number of different sources, as well as from my own clinical experience. The websites listed below have been particularly helpful and are great places to find more information about the conditions in the book. There's also a selection of some of the international charities which can help you access the support you might need to deal with your digestive symptoms.

General health websites

Each of these sites contains information about digestive disorders alongside sections on conditions affecting every other part of the body.

www.nhs.uk
The website of the UK's National Health Service, which has pages on all of the conditions mentioned in the book.

www.patient.co.uk
A website of evidence-based health advice.

www.netdoctor.co.uk
Another excellent general health resource.

www.cancerreasearchuk.org

 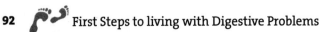

UK-based charity which researches all types of cancer, including those affecting the digestive system.

www.webmd.com
This has both a UK and US site, both of which feature interactive health information about an extensive list of conditions.

www.mayoclinic.org
The website of one of the pre-eminent healthcare providers in the USA. This site contains advice written by their clinicians and researchers.

www.bps.org.uk
This is the website of the British Psychological Society, the professional body of psychologists in the UK. It includes information on how psychological therapies can help a variety of health conditions and provides links to help find a psychologist working near you.

Websites focusing on digestive problems

www.corecharity.org.uk
Core is a charity supporting research into digestive disorders as well as providing evidence-based information for people suffering with them.

www.coeliac.org.uk
This is a charity involved in researching coeliac disease and helping those diagnosed with it. The website has loads of useful advice about the disease and some great recipe ideas for gluten-free meals.

www.aboutibs.org

The International Foundation for Functional Gastrointestinal Disorders is a US-based charity dedicated to helping people diagnosed with irritable bowel syndrome. Its website covers everything from symptoms and diagnostic tests to treatments and special diets to help settle the condition.

www.gutfoundation.com.au

This Australian charity has been set up to help prevent gastrointestinal disease by encouraging people to have better nutrition. The website discusses digestive diseases in some detail and it provides advice about how to maximize your chances of having a healthy gut.

www.cdhf.ca

The Canadian Digestive Health Foundation provides advice and support about digestive disorders. Its website again has lots of advice about the conditions covered in this book and how to enjoy a good quality of life despite having them.

Also currently available in the "First Steps" series:

First Steps out of Anxiety
Dr Kate Middleton

First Steps through Bereavement
Sue Mayfield

First Steps out of Depression
Sue Atkinson

First Steps out of Eating Disorders
Dr Kate Middleton
and Jane Smith

First Steps through the Menopause
Catherine Francis

First Steps out of Problem Drinking
John McMahon

First Steps out of Problem Gambling
Lisa Mills and Joanna Hughes

First Steps through Separation and Divorce
Penny Rich

First Steps out of Weight Problems
Catherine Francis

First Steps to living with Dementia
Dr Simon Atkins

First Steps out of Smoking
Dr Simon Atkins

First Steps through Insomnia
Dr Simon Atkins

First Steps to living with Diabetes
Dr Simon Atkins